Seth Bullock

A Captivating Guide to Deadwood's First Sheriff Who Tamed This Wild West Town and Was Later Appointed US Marshal by Theodore Roosevelt

Free Bonus from Captivating History (Available for a Limited time)

Hi History Lovers!

Now you have a chance to join our exclusive history list so you can get your first history ebook for free as well as discounts and a potential to get more history books for free! Simply visit the link below to join.

Captivatinghistory.com/ebook

Also, make sure to follow us on Facebook, Twitter and Youtube by searching for Captivating History.

Contents

INTRODUCTION 1

CHAPTER 1 - THE BIRTH OF A LEGEND 3

CHAPTER 2 - FIRST BLOOD 8

CHAPTER 3 - DEADWOOD..17

CHAPTER 4 - THE BULLOCK HOTEL.......................................32

CONCLUSION..41

HERE'S ANOTHER BOOK BY CAPTIVATING HISTORY THAT
YOU MIGHT LIKE 43

FREE BONUS FROM CAPTIVATING HISTORY (AVAILABLE FOR
A LIMITED TIME) 44

SOURCES 45

ILLUSTRATIONS 48

Introduction

Seth Bullock's name is perhaps not so legendary as that of his many contemporaries. Names like Wild Bill Hickok, Calamity Jane, and Wyatt Earp have a more fabled ring to them than simple Seth Bullock. Nonetheless, he stands out among the characters of the Old West for one simple reason: if the Wild West was a mighty predator, Seth Bullock was a lion tamer.

Bullock's life has been fictionalized in the popular television series *Deadwood*. The namesake of the show, Deadwood, South Dakota, was a lawless mining camp in the late 19th century that desperately needed a strong-hearted lawman to bring order to its rowdy streets. Bullock was its first sheriff, and he achieved law and order without killing a single enemy.

This is Bullock's most famous exploit, but he was more than just an Old West sheriff. His life was always lived to the fullest, with his seventy-one years utterly filled with his many interests and achievements. Although he became an emblem of the American West, Seth was actually born in Canada as the son of a British major. Before moving to Deadwood, he was part of the Montana Territorial Legislature, even helping to found one of the world's most famous (and earliest) national parks.

Seth was also an adept businessman, building a hotel that still stands today, founding a town, and introducing one of South Dakota's key crops. His story is filled with fascinating people, from Wild Bill Hickok to Theodore Roosevelt to his treasured friend and business partner, Solomon Star.

These names may have the ring of fiction to them, but Seth Bullock's story of integrity and dedication to the letter of the law is one that rings deeply true. It is one that served as an inspiration in a time of great lawlessness, and it is one that can serve the same purpose today.

Chapter 1 – The Birth of a Legend

Among the warmth and lushness of a Canadian midsummer, Anna Findley Bullock's screams rang through the quiet air of Amherstburg, Canada West (modern-day Ontario).

This was not her first time giving birth. Anna was a hardened Scot, and her hoarse accent rang out in her cries; like most women of the 19th century, she was well practiced in pushing out healthy babies in the most unlikely of conditions. Her marriage to a British sergeant major and an important figure in the local community had ensured that she had nothing but the best, yet at the time, the best was what would be considered almost inhumane today. Attended by an untrained midwife, sprawled in her own bed, Anna Findley Bullock was bringing her child into the world with no drugs, no sterile equipment, and no pain relief.

But as she had done before—and would do a total of at least eight times during her life—Anna made do. She brought forth a little son on July 23rd, 1849. He was born into a glorious summer and also into a life that promised brutality.

Anna knew that all too well.

* * * *

The little boy, soon named Seth, was one of eight children born to Anna and her husband, Sergeant Major George Bullock. At a time when Canada was still deep in the powerful grip of British occupation, a military man like George wielded considerable power. Native-born Canadians—both the indigenous peoples and those who descended from French and British colonists of earlier centuries—strived to loosen the terrible grasp of the British. Numerous bloody wars had been fought between the motherland and its colonists, and George had been hailed as a hero thanks to them.

In the home, however, George quickly proved to be anything but a hero to his wife and young family. While little is known about Seth Bullock's early life in Amherstburg and later Sandwich (modern-day Windsor) is that he suffered. His father was prosperous and well respected in his social circles, so Seth had no need to fear cold or hunger. There would always be books from which to learn, food on the table, and clothes on his back.

The deficiency from which young Seth suffered was a deficiency of compassion.

George was a violent man, given to fits of temper, and was deeply selfish. He was well used to power; in addition to his military accomplishments, he was elected as county treasurer in the 1850s. And he held that power over his family in a reign of pure terror. All of his children feared him. Perhaps even his wife as well, although she faded quickly from Seth's world when he was still very young. Anna's staunch Scottish blood had stood her in good stead through eight children, her marriage to the violent George, and many a Canadian winter. But it failed her at last sometime before 1860, leaving Seth alone with his siblings and his father.

One can only imagine that little Seth must have lived in fear. Even the tiniest of mistakes could spark an outburst of rage. In an age when the odd spanking was the norm, Seth suffered more than most.

George was unafraid of heartily beating his children, and Seth was no exception. Each time he made the smallest error, Seth felt his father's wrath physically.

George grew abusive enough that in 1858, when Seth was nine, he decided that he could no longer tolerate living with his cruel father. He fled from the home, but his runaway attempt didn't last for very long. Seth had nowhere else to go. And while freedom certainly appealed to him, the Canadian wilderness then surrounding Sandwich was no place for a nine-year-old boy to survive alone. He returned, dejected. This was the first of many times that Seth ran away from home. For the next five years, he would continue to run away any time the opportunity presented itself.

In 1860, however, Seth was suddenly and dramatically liberated from his father's iron fist—and, at the same time, catapulted into a world of total uncertainty. George had been enjoying his stint as county treasurer a little more than he should have. In fact, evidence was found that funds were missing from the treasury, causing George's superiors to become immediately suspicious that he was feathering his own nest at the county's expense. He was fired from his position as treasurer.

Instead of facing what he'd done, George showed his true colors shortly afterward. Like most cruel bullies, George was a total coward. Despite the fact that he still had many children at home—a few of Seth's older siblings had gotten married by this point—George regarded his own freedom and safety to be more important than his children's welfare. He simply disappeared from Sandwich, leaving his children all alone, and fled to Detroit, Michigan.

While Detroit was just a few miles away from Sandwich (now Windsor), George may as well have been living in another world. The United States of America had been an independent country for decades, and while George wasn't physically distant from the children, he had practically disappeared from their lives completely.

Eleven-year-old Seth and the others were left to fend for themselves. While this meant that Seth was finally free from the iron fist of his father, it also meant that he had to find some way to survive. Just a few years after George disappeared, it all became too much for Seth. His older sister, Agnes, was getting ready to go and live in Montana by then, and even though it was more than a thousand miles away, the teenage Seth made the trek to live with her. It was his first taste of the West, and it was love at first sight.

By the time Seth was fourteen years old, his childhood home had been sold off to the highest bidder. George had abandoned his children to the extent that he didn't even bother to continue paying the mortgage on the home that housed them. The house was claimed by the bank and auctioned, and nothing was left of the unhappy Bullock family that had once been so prominent in Sandwich.

For Seth Bullock, however, this was just the beginning. Despite his rebellious escapes as a child, Seth was nonetheless developing a keen sense of justice and a keen desire to avoid unnecessary violence. His father had inspired him to become someone important and respected in the community but also someone who could rule with a moderate hand. And in the future, that was the destiny Seth Bullock would fulfill.

* * * *

While the teenage Seth Bullock was growing familiar with the wild landscapes of the West, an all-too-familiar conflict was spreading farther and farther into the wilderness of South Dakota—a wilderness whose fate was inextricably linked to Seth's.

The stark yet lovely Black Hills of South Dakota had been the ancestral home of many different Native American tribes for untold centuries. While the word "hills" might conjure visions of a gently rolling landscape clothed in green, the Black Hills were a harsh landscape. With steep, rocky cliffs, deep gulches, and wild mountain streams, they were a gloriously pristine wilderness that was home to a vast array of wildlife, including great herds of buffalo.

These buffalo shaped the diet, culture, and even religion of one of the most prominent local tribes: the Lakota, also known as the Teton Sioux. Before the 19th century, the Lakota had been in sole control of a vast tract of land populated by the buffalo herds that provided them with food and leather. This nomadic tribe would roam across the Black Hills freely, hunting and fishing as they willed, loving and worshiping as their culture decreed.

But the Black Hills were rich in something other than buffalo. The streams there ran pure, clean, and cold—and they were speckled with gold. There was gold in the dirt, too, and the white man's incessant hunger for this metal would eventually bring him onto the doorstep of the Lakota.

This was a tragedy for the Lakota tribe. Not only did the Black Hills provide them with resources essential to their survival, but the hills were also sacred in their religion. To them, the colonists might as well have been pillaging a church building. Spats broke out between the colonists and the Lakota, and with the colonists vastly outnumbered by their Native American counterparts, a bloody war broke out in the 1860s.

In 1868, the US government finally decided to put an end to the fighting. The Treaty of Fort Laramie was signed, giving full possession of the Black Hills to the Lakota tribe. It seemed peace would come at last. But the Lakota had no use for the gold that ran so richly in their hills and streams, and the colonists cared little who the land belonged to: all they wanted was gold.

By 1870, hundreds of miners had set up their hovels on Lakota territory, trespassing, squatting, and then pillaging the sacred land for gold. Tensions began to rise. Trouble was on the way.

Chapter 2 – First Blood

Illustration I: Seth Bullock, photographed in 1893. This photograph now hangs in Theodore Roosevelt's birthplace, a National Historic Site.

https://commons.wikimedia.org/wiki/File:SethBullock.jpg

Agnes Bullock, one of Seth's three sisters, had fallen in love with an explorer: Lieutenant Frederick F. Kislingbury.

Frederick was only two years older than Seth, but he was far more traveled. Born in England, Frederick had moved to the US as a child and served during the American Civil War at the tender age of seventeen. By the time he married Agnes, he was only around twenty-one years old, but he was already a veteran of America's bloodiest war.

He was also a resident of Helena, Montana, which was about 1,700 miles from the town where Seth had grown up. Still, this didn't seem to be a problem for either Agnes or Seth. They likely wanted to put as much space as possible between them and their abusive past, so when Agnes married Frederick, Seth was only too eager to come right along and leave his life in Canada behind.

Seth's older sister, Agnes, was used to caring for him. Their father had disappeared seven years earlier, and their mother had died so long ago; Agnes was the only real parent Seth had left. Bringing him to Helena with her was a logical choice in her mind. And it was a choice that would change the path of Seth's life forever, as well as the history of a small but notorious South Dakota town. However, Agnes herself would not live to see most of Seth's fame. She died in 1878, after which Frederick married her younger sister, Jessie. Jessie would become a widow in 1884 when Frederick tragically died (and was probably cannibalized by his own starving, dying comrades) during an expedition to the Arctic Circle.

After the long journey to Montana, which was likely traveled by steam train the majority of the way, Seth was introduced to a whole new world. The long rocky beaches and verdant maples of Sandwich were replaced by the wild prairies and blue mountainsides of the West, and Seth had never known such freedom. While he found that he had a knack for business, quickly settling into becoming a tradesman and auctioneer in Helena, Seth's passion lay with the nearby wilderness.

The young man took to exploring the vast tracts of mountains, prairies, lakes, and rivers surrounding Helena, and he had a love for nature that was very different from most young men who moved out West. In an age when the majority of young white male colonists were obsessed with cutting trees, digging up hillsides in search of gold, and building towns on previously undisturbed lands, Seth recognized the wilderness itself held an intrinsic value that went far beyond the resources it could offer a growing nation.

Among the tall pine trees, with the cries of wild wolves echoing in the woods and mighty grizzly bears stalking the salmon-rich rivers, Seth found a timeless beauty and power. He was aware that the ever-hungry beast of westward expansion was swallowing up endless tracts of once-pristine wilderness. Wildlife and wild places were not so much being tamed as they were being utterly destroyed. Seth felt a deep urgency not to let that happen to the area he loved.

By 1870, Seth had left Agnes's home and built a life for himself at the age of twenty-one. He was a successful auctioneer and was becoming a respected figure in his local community. At this point, his dream of going into politics and becoming a leader in his community started to materialize.

Montana, at the time, was not yet a state; it would only become one in 1889. However, it was a US territory, complete with its own territorial legislature and a territorial senate. Seth, a Republican, had his sights set on being elected to the legislature and ran for it in 1870. While his bid proved to be unsuccessful, he ran for the territorial senate the following year, and this time, he achieved his goal. He was elected.

One of Seth's duties around this time was to ride on the local Helena fire engine. Firefighting in the 1870s was very different from what we know today; firefighters were almost always volunteers, and they carried their fire engines around by hand or drove them around by a team of horses. When wooden buildings caught on fire, they were slow-burning—in sharp contrast with the fires of today, where homes are outfitted with gas and electricity—and most of Seth's work likely consisted of salvaging things from burning houses. Still, it quickly made him a hero in his community.

One of his most important contributions as a senator involved the landscape that he had grown to love during his years in Helena. That pristine wilderness was under increasing threat from the ever-encroaching, gold-hungry Americans, and Seth knew that something drastic would have to be done to conserve even a piece of the American West. In an era long before nature conservation would become a buzzword, Seth proposed a daring new idea. He wanted a huge area that stretched over Montana, Wyoming, and Idaho to be declared not simply a state park—which Yosemite, nearby, already was—but a national park. A place that would be safe from encroachment forever.

Seth's daring idea was accepted by the territorial legislature, and Montana Territory worked hard to get the proposal pushed through to the federal level. Ultimately, it was successful. In March 1872, during Seth's last year as a Montana senator, the world's very first national park was established. It was named Yellowstone National Park, and it remains the oldest national park in the world, protecting over 3,000 square miles of wilderness, nearly 400 animal species, and the famous geyser Old Faithful.

If it wasn't for Seth Bullock, we might not have a Yellowstone today. In fact, considering how instrumental Yellowstone has been in the conservation of some of America's most critically endangered species, some of the continent's most amazing animals might have gone extinct without the park. These include icons like the grizzly bear, gray wolf, pika, and Canada lynx. These animals have Seth Bullock, at least in part, to thank for their existence. Without his vision of preserving the area he explored as a young man, they might have been hunted to extinction.

* * * *

Although Seth's stint in the Montana Territorial Senate ended in 1872, his interest in politics and community leadership was far from over. Instead of waning, his interest grew. While he still enjoyed trading and making business deals, the now twenty-three-year-old Seth was very interested in being a leader in his community—a real leader, one with integrity and firmness, very unlike how his corrupt father had been.

It was easy, then, for Seth to be elected as the county sheriff in 1873. As the sheriff of Lewis and Clark County, Seth was given the unenviable task of establishing law and order in the Wild West. The county was only eight years old at the time, and while Helena had been fairly civilized, Seth now found himself governing a scattering of mining towns that were filled with the wildest and most lawless characters the West could offer.

Faced with such a daunting task, many Old West sheriffs became unspeakably violent. Long before the term "police brutality" was ever coined, these sheriffs sometimes acted with wanton violence, abusing their power and killing, imprisoning, and even torturing with abandon. Seth Bullock was determined not to be one of those sheriffs. He'd tasted enough violence at the hard fist of his father, and he knew that there had to be a better way.

Still, Seth had a keen eye for justice and a willingness to do whatever was necessary to ensure what he considered to be fair treatment in the eyes of the sometimes-brutal Western law. It was inevitable that Seth would come to blows with some criminal or another. That criminal turned out to be a dangerous character named Clell Watson.

In the Old West, horse theft was considered to be one of the most serious crimes that a man could commit. In a time when raping a Native American woman carried little penalty, stealing horses could get you hanged. While the injustice is obvious to the modern reader, it is true that horses were essential to businesses and to survival in the West, making them extremely valuable. The law decreed that horse thieves had to be prosecuted, and Seth was determined to follow the law to the letter.

So, when Seth came upon Watson stealing a horse, he was quick to make his presence known. Watson briskly drew his firearm, and despite his aversion to unnecessary violence, Seth had no scruples about defending himself and carrying out what he perceived to be his duty. Gunfire was exchanged, and blood was drawn. Seth Bullock was wounded for the first time in action. However, he succeeded in his mission. Clell Watson was arrested and sentenced to hanging.

The hanging would take place publicly, as most executions of the time did, but it turned out that Watson was quite popular among the local population. They swarmed around the scaffold, ready to do violence and rescue their thieving companion. The noose was already around Watson's neck, but the executioner's courage deserted him. He abandoned his prisoner and fled, but before Watson could go free, Seth leaped into action. Even though he was wounded, Seth seized a shotgun and chased off the mob, then pulled the lever himself. Clell Watson dropped through the trapdoor to his death. No members of the mob were injured, but they had heard the message from Seth loud and clear: he was not going to allow anyone to stand in the way of the United States law. Seth Bullock was going to uphold everything that he stood for, even if it meant putting himself in life-threatening danger.

* * * *

Seth Bullock's stint as the sheriff of Lewis and Clark County would continue until 1875. In 1874, the handsome young sheriff married Martha Eccles, a woman he had been in love with for years. Martha had fallen in love with a lost boy; now, she was married to a tall, strong sheriff with a thick mustache and steely eyes.

Shortly after Seth and Martha were married, history was once again in the making 500 miles away in the Black Hills of South Dakota.

The Lakota were still arguing against the squatters and trespassers mining on their land, but theirs was a losing battle. The United States government was far more concerned with the gold that these illegal miners were discovering than they were with the cultural significance that the Black Hills had for the waning Lakota tribe. Thus, a blind eye was turned as miners continued to push farther and farther into the Black Hills, looking for gold.

While many miners would find themselves as penniless after their efforts as before them, there were a few that struck lucky. One such was John B. Pearson. A desperate miner like all the others, Pearson was scrambling through a deep gulch in the hills, its cliffs sheer and littered with dead trees. Through the thick tangles of dead branches, he could hear the quick hiss of a fast-running stream at the bottom.

It was a beautiful stream, pure and cold like all the others. But unlike all the others, this one's floor flashed with real gold.

It was 1875, and by this point, around 800 miners were squatting on Lakota land in the Black Hills. When word got around of the gold that Pearson had found, these miners didn't waste any time flocking to the ravine, which was quickly dubbed Deadwood Gulch. Tents sprang up overnight like mushrooms; in a matter of weeks, the wilderness had become a mining camp, filled with rowdy men hungry for gold.

The disorganized array of tents and shanties multiplied as more and more gold was drawn from the stream. It became obvious that there was a real opportunity here, and the more gold there was, the more men came. They started to live permanently in the gulch, and it wasn't long before men did as men will: they began to drink, gamble, steal, seek after prostitutes, and kill one another over seemingly trivial arguments.

By 1876, Deadwood had become a mining camp, and it was the most notorious camp in all the West. There were almost no families here, just a great restless mass of wild men. Some say that a murder was committed every single day of the first year of Deadwood's existence; another shocking statistic is that nine out of every ten women living in Deadwood was a prostitute.

One of the men who played a key role in making Deadwood so dangerous was an Iowan-born businessman by the name of Ellis Albert Swearengen. He would eventually go by a name that became an outlaw legend: Al Swearengen. While he appeared to be an educated, sophisticated, and cultured man at first glance, the truth was that Al was one of the most dangerous men in the West.

Born just a few weeks before Seth, Al grew up and worked in Iowa, but he quickly saw a business opportunity in the booming West. In the spring of 1876, Deadwood was undoubtedly the place to be. Its hills were rich with gold, but it wasn't gold that Al was after. Gold was hard to find. But gold miners were a dime a dozen; they swarmed through the gulch, filling it with their tents and shanties, and Al knew that there was money to be made off them.

At the time, Deadwood had a ramshackle saloon and not much else. In fact, there wasn't even a hardware store. Hundreds of men were crammed into the miserable gulch with no way of distracting themselves from the hardships of frontier life. Al decided that there was money to be made in entertaining them.

Just seven days after his arrival in Deadwood with his wife, Nettie, Al's first business opportunity was up and running. He had started a dance hall in Deadwood, and it proved to be unbelievably popular. Soon, Al expanded the dance hall into a tiny saloon named the Cricket Saloon. Here, he provided men with as much beer as they could drink and as many women as they could paw at.

Al's own woman led an absolutely miserable life. Al treated her like property, which was not unusual for the time, but he also abused her physically. Nettie was being bruised and battered just like any of the hapless prostitutes that were trapped in Al's service at the Cricket. And with a town swarming with restless young men whose morals had been degraded by the hardships of the frontier, the prostitutes' lives were nothing less than miserable.

And this was only the beginning for Al Swearengen. He would grow more and more bold, his establishment more and more seedy and violent, over the next three months. After all, there was no one around to stop him.

Deadwood was about as lawless as it is possible to be. But not for long.

A new sheriff was coming to town.

Chapter 3 – Deadwood

Illustration II: Deadwood

*https://commons.wikimedia.org/wiki/File:Grabill_-
_Deadwood,_Dakota._A_part_of_the_city_from_Forest_Hill.jpg*

Although Seth would later become known as the man who tamed Deadwood, when he first traveled to the booming town, he wasn't going as a lawman.

While Seth had spent several years working hard in leadership positions, establishing Yellowstone National Park and helping to tame the corner of the Wild West dubbed Lewis and Clark County, he was by no means neglecting his other major strength: his keen business acumen. Having established himself as a trader and an auctioneer in Helena, Seth was always looking out for other ways to develop his business and become even more of an entrepreneur. One man who was instrumental in his business career was Solomon "Sol" Star.

Sol and Seth had a lot in common. For one thing, Sol, too, had grown up almost without parents. Five years Seth's elder, Sol was born just before the Christmas of 1840 in Bavaria. At the time, this state in the south of Germany was an independent kingdom, an absolute monarchy torn apart by revolutions in the changing political climate of the 19th century. Sol's mother and father realized that their son didn't have a future there. When he was only ten years old, he was sent on the long voyage to the United States of America to live with his maternal uncle, Joseph Friedlander.

Joseph lived in Ohio and worked as a merchant, running a busy store. Young Sol, robbed of his family and everything he held dear, possibly also struggling with a language barrier, was nonetheless quick to pick up on the trade. He had a keen sense of business and was quickly intrigued by his uncle's ideas. It wasn't long before the young Bavarian immigrant became an important member of his community.

He moved west to Montana in 1865 at the age of twenty-five to start up a store of his own. Even though the journey was more than a thousand miles, and Sol was starting up in an entirely foreign state, he threw himself into the task with great fervor. By 1872, Sol had become involved in politics as well. President Ulysses S. Grant appointed him to the Land Office of Montana that year. It was the same year that Seth was serving on the territorial legislature.

Since Helena was the territorial capital of Montana, Seth and Sol inevitably would meet and work together, and the two young men quickly struck up something more than just a business relationship. Since they shared so many interests and even elements of their childhood, it wasn't long before Seth and Sol were firm friends. Their strong leadership capabilities and their good business sense made them a formidable pair.

Somewhere around 1873, soon after Seth pulled the lever on Clell Watson and had established himself as the county sheriff, Seth and Sol decided to enter into business together. With booming mining towns and growing ranches all around them, they were quick to settle on a lucrative opportunity: they'd build a hardware store. Everyone in the area needed hardware for something or another, and soon, Seth and Sol were running a successful little store.

But as Seth's tenure as the sheriff of Lewis and Clark County drew to a close, the two men threw themselves into their business, and they began to realize that even better opportunities lay much farther afield. In particular, South Dakota was absolutely thriving. Now that gold had been found in the Black Hills, men were pouring into the territory at an amazing rate, and boom towns were springing up all over the once-perfect wilderness. There was no Yellowstone National Park for South Dakota; there was just a constant invasion of people.

And the town that was the most lucrative of all was Deadwood.

Like Al Swearengen, though, Seth and Sol were both uninterested in mining for gold. Instead, they recognized that thousands of people in Deadwood were eventually going to realize that they needed more than just mining tools, alcohol, and prostitutes. They would begin to build houses, and they would eventually come to need all ordinary equipment and household items that Seth and Sol had been selling in Helena for years.

For Seth, it was a bittersweet moment when he and his friend decided to seek their fortune in Deadwood with a new store. His marriage to Martha was important to him, and they had just had their first child, a little girl called Margaret. He had striven to be the father to her that George never was to him. But now, it meant moving to Deadwood and forging a better future for all of them. Perhaps the Wild West really could be tamed; perhaps Martha and Margaret could come and join him soon.

With a heart heavy yet excited for the future, Seth set off on the long trail to Deadwood. Today, the 500 miles between Helena and Deadwood can be covered in eight hours by car, but in the summer of 1876, the only way that Seth and Sol could travel between the two towns, laden as they were with their wares, was by ox wagon. It was a long, slow journey, and they rumbled on through the summer heat and the many dangers that stalked the West—from angry Native Americans robbed of their homes to plain old highwaymen looking for their next victims.

On the first day of August 1876, Seth Bullock and Sol Star reached Deadwood, exhausted from the trail. Neither of them could possibly know that they would forever shape the character and future of the wild mining camp. Still, despite the long journey that lay behind them, Seth and Sol wasted absolutely no time in getting down to business.

Deadwood was, at the time, filled with young single men who had come to the West with romantic ideas and a thirst for gold, and their mining camp certainly reflected their priorities. There were plenty of pans for panning gold in the stream, plenty of women, and plenty of booze. However, the supply of basic hygiene products was pitiful. Most of these men were living in tents; they probably hadn't had a bath (except for dipping their feet into the stream) in months, and they smelt like it. Worst of all, even though flushing toilets had become common in more civilized areas around the 1850s, there were none of these to be had in Deadwood. Even a latrine was considered a luxury. Most men were hankering simply for a chamber pot.

Luckily for the men and for their business, Seth and Sol had come prepared with a whole wagonload of chamber pots. Still, they hadn't brought enough to sell one to every desperate Deadwood resident. Instead, they auctioned the chamber pots off to the highest bidder, raking in cash on their very first night in Deadwood. It may not have been a glamorous start to their new business venture, but it was definitely a promising one.

The duo, however, would soon learn that they weren't in Montana anymore. Deadwood was a whole new world, a place whose reality lived up to the West's notorious reputation. The very day after Seth and Sol arrived, an appalling murder took place in Deadwood's No. 10 Saloon. The murderer would come perilously close to getting off scot-free, and although Seth didn't know it yet, this killing would be the start of the most illustrious part of his career as a lawman.

* * * *

James Butler "Wild Bill" Hickok might have been born in Illinois, but he would become a true legend of the Wild West.

Wild Bill grew up simply as James, and he spent most of his early life farming peacefully, but he always had a penchant for firearms. His skill as a gunslinger was tested early on when he moved to Kansas in 1855 to claim a homestead and start his own farm. The years of 1855 and 1856 were a terrible time in Kansas Territory. With tensions over the issue of slavery erupting all over the United States, new territories like Kansas were deeply divided over whether they would be a slave or free state. Many pushed to uphold slavery, seeing dollar signs as they considered the potential of the already-lucrative West being tamed by unpaid labor. Others believed in abolition and wanted the new territories to be free. Kansas became a center for conflict over this issue, with pioneers turning on one another. Although it would be another six years before the American Civil War officially began, the period known as "Bleeding Kansas" was a gruesome foretaste of the slaughter to come.

James Hickok was only eighteen years old at the time, but he did what thousands of other young men in Kansas did. He took up his gun, and he fought for what he believed in: freedom for all men.

He emerged from Bleeding Kansas not as James Butler but as Bill, taking his father's name now that he felt like a man. He had garnered a reputation as being a terrifyingly accurate marksman and a fearless gunfighter, and it was a reputation that would only grow in the years to come. He served as a constable in Kansas for a time before relocating to Nebraska, where he chose a quieter life for a short while, becoming a stockman at Rock Creek Station.

If Bill was hoping to find peace and tranquility at Rock Creek, his hopes were dashed. As he went about his work tending animals, his neighbor, David McCanles, decided that young Bill was a target. He started to mock him, giving him the derogatory nickname of "Duck Bill." This may have been rooted in his suspicions that his mistress was cheating on him with Bill. This suspicion was not groundless, as Bill was indeed sleeping with David McCanles's mistress.

Bill appears to have taken McCanles's mocking with good humor, or at least without violence. All that changed on July 12th, 1861. With the Civil War in its infancy, conflict was erupting in the East. It had not yet affected Nebraska, but blood was nonetheless shed at Rock Creek Station on that dark day.

David McCanles came looking for trouble. Accompanied by two older men and his son, then a preteen boy, McCanles swaggered up to the station manager and started arguing with him about payment for a piece of land. His real target sat inside the station behind a curtain, minding his own business but ever alert—and, as always, armed. Bleeding Kansas had taught Bill to always be ready for a fight.

Finally, McCanles announced to the station manager what his real intent had been in coming to the station. He demanded that the station manager step aside and allow him to assault Bill, calling him "Duck Bill" as usual.

Behind the curtain, Bill heard every word.

"There'll be one less [of you] if you try that," he said, with rather more profanity than is recorded here.

David McCanles considered Bill's words to be an empty threat and very quickly found out that they weren't. He rushed at the curtain, ready to pluck it aside and kill Bill, but he never got the chance. Through the curtain, Bill fired off a shot that echoed across Nebraska and into the annals of history. The bullet punched into McCanles's chest, and he stumbled out of the station, white-faced and dying.

His poor little son, only twelve years old, was appalled at the sight of his bleeding father. He ran to catch him as he collapsed, just in time for McCanles to breathe his last.

Outraged that their leader was dead, the other two men who had accompanied McCanles charged upon Bill with their weapons drawn. They started firing, and soon, the station was filled with the blast and whine of bullets.

When the shooting stopped, one of McCanles's two companions was dead. The other had been wounded by Bill and ran out of the station, after which Bill's allies, coming to help after hearing the sound of gunfire, killed him.

It wasn't long before the newspapers were filled with the exploits of the great gunslinger, calling him the name that would go down in history: "Wild Bill" Hickok. And while some of the accounts of Wild Bill's exploits were most certainly exaggerated, it is absolutely true that he was one of the best gunslingers the West had ever known.

Despite his nickname of "wild," Bill generally kept to the right side of the law. During the American Civil War, he fought with the Union Army, first as a scout and then later—possibly—as a spy in the Confederacy. His stint in the Union Army is veiled in secrecy, lending credence to the theory that he worked as a spy.

After the Civil War, Bill was still not tired of fighting. In fact, just months after the war ended, he was a part of a gunfight so classically Old Western that it almost doesn't feel real.

Bill was in Springfield, Missouri, at the time, drifting as he waited for the war to end and undoubtedly up to no good. He'd had a falling out with one of his friends, Davis Tutt, as both young men had fallen in love with the same woman. Things were only made worse between Bill and Davis when Bill lost a poker game to Davis and failed to pay his debt. Davis pinched Bill's treasured pocket watch and then proudly strutted around the Springfield town square wearing it.

This angered Bill, who was now twenty-eight years old. He warned Davis repeatedly to stop wearing the watch, which Davis completely ignored. Why would he listen to Bill? He had won the watch fairly in a poker game, and it was his property.

Bill didn't see it that way. And, back in 1865, there was only one sure way to settle this argument: a duel to the death.

The duel took place in the town square, and just the description of the event fills one's mind with Ennio Morricone's iconic music, the theme from the 1966 film *The Good, The Bad and the Ugly*. The people in the square parted to make way for the two gunslingers, and total silence fell as Wild Bill and Davis faced one another about seventy-five feet apart.

Accounts vary on exactly what happened next. Both men were armed. Both men drew their weapons. The accounts agree that Wild Bill was quicker on the draw. Some say he shot first; others say that he stood, pistol in hand, waiting for Davis to fire. Davis's shot missed completely, and before he could shoot again, Wild Bill raised his gun.

As one of the witnesses said, "Bill never shoots at the same man twice." Davis died with Wild Bill's bullet in his heart. Wild Bill was tried for manslaughter, but for better or worse, the authorities at the time reasoned that it had been a fair fight, and they let him go.

In general, despite his murder of a man over a pocket watch, Wild Bill was seen as an astute lawman and a pillar of strength in the Wild West. He became the sheriff in Hays City, Kansas, and served there for many years to tame the outlaws of the region. His status as a legendary gunman and uncompromising sheriff spread all over the West, and his name became synonymous with the old gunslingers of the American West.

It all came crashing down for Wild Bill in 1871. He was raiding a saloon in Hays City on suspicion of illegal activity taking place there (as it generally did in most saloons), and as he and his deputy took on the saloon owner and his cronies, bullets were flying, smoke filled the air, and utter chaos broke loose. For the first and final time, Wild Bill lost his head in a gunfight. He fired at the nearest man, killing him the way he always did, with one or two quick shots to the chest.

When the smoke cleared, it turned out that the dead man was no outlaw. It was Mike Williams, Wild Bill's trusted deputy.

That was Wild Bill's final gunfight. He never drew his weapon in anger again, unable to forget his accidental killing of an innocent friend. With no other skills, Wild Bill turned to target shooting, traveling around for a few years with Buffalo Bill Cody in his famous Wild West show. He entertained the crowds with his great feats of marksmanship.

Even though Wild Bill shot only at targets for the cheers of the crowd, even that wouldn't last for long. Glaucoma stole his legendary eyesight, robbing him of the one great skill he'd ever had. By 1876, Wild Bill was almost blind. Despite the fact that he was not yet forty years old, Wild Bill was a has-been—a down-and-out, destitute relic of a once-legendary lawman.

He came to Deadwood in desperation, hoping to find some way to survive there, and he fell back on poker for his existence. Everything had been taken from Wild Bill. He had no career, no eyesight, and no real skills. All he had was desperation and the sad knowledge that, at the age of thirty-nine, his glory days were behind him.

Still, Wild Bill might have had some kind of a future if it hadn't been brutally taken from him in a senseless act of appalling violence. In fact, despite his destitution and sad prospects, Wild Bill had just gotten married to Agnes Thatcher Lake. Agnes was a force to be reckoned with in and of herself, as she ran her own circus and also performed in it as a tightrope walker, lion tamer, and horse rider. After several chance encounters throughout the years, Agnes and Wild Bill were married on March 7th, 1876. After a two-week honeymoon in Cincinnati, Ohio, during which the two appeared to be thoroughly in love, Wild Bill left for South Dakota.

And he never returned.

Although Wild Bill had ostensibly gone to South Dakota to seek a fortune, there is little evidence of his mining activities. Instead, Wild Bill had become nothing but a gambler, trying to scrape together enough money to be reunited with his wife by playing poker.

On the morning of August 2nd, 1876 (a morning when many Deadwood men were awakening to their glorious new chamber pots from Seth Bullock and Sol Star), Wild Bill was heading to the No. 10 Saloon in Deadwood as he usually did. He sat down with his back to the door, a seat he typically avoided, to play a poker match with some other local gamblers.

He was looking down at his hand, noting that he had two black aces and two black eights. This hand is known to this day as the "dead man's hand" because of what happened next.

The door of the saloon swung open. No one took any notice of the armed young cowboy who walked into the saloon. It was Deadwood, after all; literally everyone was armed. Everyone continued to mind their own cards and beer as the young man walked up to Wild Bill, drew his pistol, and shot the gunslinger in the back of the head.

Wild Bill was dead before his head hit the poker table, splattering blood over the game. Chaos broke loose in the saloon, but the shooter, Jack McCall, was not particularly concerned. He walked right out of the saloon and left. Agnes was made a widow not even six months after she'd become a wife.

* * * *

Wild Bill had lived through so many dazzling exploits and gained such a great reputation as a warrior and lawman, yet his death was absolutely senseless and brutal. However, it was more than just a terribly tragic end to Wild Bill's life. It was a horrifying example of how lawless Deadwood had become, that someone could simply walk up and shoot an ex-sheriff and national legend in the back of the head, then walk right out again.

McCall was detained shortly after the shooting of Wild Bill. As Seth and Sol were finding their feet in the new town, Deadwood was setting up an impromptu camp court. Somehow, despite the fact that McCall had murdered Wild Bill in front of many witnesses, he was found not guilty and was allowed to walk free. Such was the extent of the lawlessness that held Deadwood in its carnal grip.

Ultimately, however, McCall's acquittal proved as a wake-up call for South Dakota authorities. Believing that he was invincible after his acquittal, McCall, who had shot Bill due to a perceived insult the day before the shooting, started to brag all around the territory that he had courageously taken on and killed the famous Wild Bill Hickok. It did not seem to occur to McCall that his act had been one of unbelievable cowardice and cruelty. All he'd really done was to walk up to an unarmed, destitute old gambler and take his life from behind at point-blank range.

McCall's boasting finally got the attention of the authorities, and he was recaptured more than six months after the murder in March 1877. This time, he was tried in front of a real court, which obviously found him guilty. McCall was hanged. His foolish act had brought about the premature and violent ending of not one life but two.

* * * *

Seth Bullock must have been appalled to hear of the killing of Wild Bill. While Seth was no edgy gunslinger like Wild Bill, as Seth's adherence to the law was far more rigid (it is difficult to imagine him killing a poker player over a pocket watch), he must have nonetheless felt a connection to Wild Bill since they had both been sheriffs. And it must also have been sobering to realize how easily one could lose their life in Deadwood.

To make matters even worse, one month after McCall was finally hanged for his crimes, Al Swearengen decided to expand his booming business. He had more sketchy business deals than we will probably ever know about, and most of them involved prostitution in some way or another. The vast majority of the women of Deadwood were working for Al Swearengen, forced to bed one reckless miner after the other. Al didn't care about the poor girls suffering in his Cricket Saloon. All he wanted was to make money, and he was making piles of it as a pimp.

On April 7th, 1877, Al opened the biggest front yet for his prostitution ring: the Gem Variety Theater. On the outside, the Gem appeared to be just that, a rare jewel of culture in the Wild West. There was beautiful wallpaper, a dance floor, and entertainment that appeared fairly civilized at first glance. But that was just the literal front of the theater building. Behind it, prostitutes were waiting, propositioning men from behind the bar because they had no other choice. The penalty for refusing to obey Al's orders was physical punishment.

Between the McCall debacle and the Gem Variety Theater, crime spiked wildly in Deadwood, and the authorities realized that enough was enough. What Deadwood really needed was a sheriff—a stern-eyed, iron-fisted lawman. The once-lovely wilderness of the Black Hills was now marred by the truly untamed portion of the Wild West, that of the animal savagery existing in the hearts of men. Someone needed to scare that right out of them. Someone who wouldn't get sucked into corruption. Someone who wouldn't place a single toe on the wrong side of the law.

Someone like Seth Bullock.

At the time, Sol and Seth had progressed from running a general and hardware store out of a tent to purchasing an actual lot on the corner of Deadwood's main street. At first, they could only build a false front for their shop, but as the months went on, Seth and Sol were beginning to prove that it was possible to make good money in the West without resorting to illegal activities. The Star and Bullock Hardware Store was booming, and it grew into a building that attracted plenty of customers every day.

Seth was working hard at his business, but he was also acutely aware that there was no way he could bring Martha and Margaret to Deadwood, not with the likes of Al Swearengen controlling the town. So, when Governor John Pennington, who was in charge of Dakota Territory, approached him, asking if he would serve temporarily as Deadwood's appointed sheriff, Seth eagerly agreed. It was March, shortly after Jack McCall's trial.

Interestingly enough, Seth would never be elected as the sheriff of Deadwood. That honor belonged to Democrat John J. Manning, who was elected in November 1877 and would serve two two-year terms, both times defeating Seth Bullock in the election. Seth only served as the sheriff of Lawrence County (which included Deadwood) for a matter of months. But a few months was enough for Seth to whip the wild town into shape.

As the sheriff of Deadwood and already one of its most prominent residents, Seth held a considerable amount of power. His decisive action during his gunfight with Clell Watson had already proven him to be a formidable fighter, yet in the nine months that Seth served as the sheriff of Deadwood, he never killed anyone in a gunfight.

Somehow, Seth Bullock tamed the town of Deadwood without any of the frontier justice that characterized the careers of many Western lawmen of his era. While executions undoubtedly would have taken place—Seth would have been raised to consider these as a form of justice—there were no gruesome gun battles during which outlaws were shot and killed, no ugly murders or duels simply to make an example out of a criminal or to make a spectacle out of Seth's gunslinger skills. He held power just like his father, George, had; but unlike George, who thought nothing of brutally beating an innocent child, Seth was aware of the weight of responsibility that this power gave him. And despite his lack of brutality, Seth tamed Deadwood in nine months.

He made several of Deadwood's more respectable citizens into sheriff's deputies, and he worked with them to systematically uproot the crime that had grown so deep into the very identity of the town.

The one nemesis that Seth never conquered, unfortunately, was Al Swearengen. Despite numerous confrontations over the years, Al somehow clung to the Gem Variety Theater and continued to run it as a brothel for the ever-eager string of customers with which the gold mines provided him. The fact that Seth Bullock never put a stop to the Gem's operations was a terrible tragedy for the prostitutes working in it. Many of them had been practically kidnapped from their homes, as they had been desperate women from the overpopulated East, attracted to Deadwood by advertisements Al placed in newspapers promising lucrative job opportunities as "waitresses" and "actresses." The women would then find themselves trapped in prostitution, and while there is little evidence to suggest that they were actual sex slaves, they certainly didn't have many other options besides staying and working at the Gem. There was a reason why Seth had not yet brought Martha and Margaret to Deadwood. It was a dangerous place for women, even more so outside the Gem than within it, and there were no opportunities for women to find respectable work. Many of them had spent their last penny getting to Deadwood. They had no choice but to stay at the Gem, and for as long as they stayed, they would be beaten for any perceived transgression. These bruised, beaten, hollow-eyed girls waited in vain for Seth to save them. It can be assumed that this was not for lack of trying, but whether he didn't have enough power or resources, or for whatever other reason, Seth never did get Al Swearengen to leave town.

Nonetheless, except for the den of vice that the Gem had become, by the time John J. Manning was sworn in as the county sheriff, Deadwood had changed. It was now safe enough that Seth Bullock could have his wife and little girl finally reunite with him in South Dakota. They came to join him in his now-booming business with Sol, and they were able to walk the streets fearlessly thanks to Seth's efforts in reforming the town.

As for Al Swearengen, he might have evaded Seth, but he eventually got what was coming to him. The Gem Variety Theater burned down twice in 1879, yet this was no major setback for Al; there was so much money to be made in his cruel line of work that he just built bigger and better theaters after each fire. Some estimates of the Gem's profits run as high as $10,000 a night—a huge sum even by modern standards, let alone in the 19th century.

Ultimately, the Gem burned down again in 1899, and Al finally got out of Deadwood. He returned to the East for a time before moving to Denver, Colorado, in 1904. It was in the streets there that he was struck and killed with a blunt object. His twin brother, Lemuel, had been shot in a similar manner a short while before; it is suspected that Al had always been the target of a hit from one of the many, many people he had harmed.

Chapter 4 – The Bullock Hotel

Illustration III: The Bullock Hotel today

By 1881, although Seth was no longer the sheriff of Deadwood and the most famous part of his life was over, he was certainly by no means done living. In fact, Seth was really just getting started.

His famous stint as the sheriff of Deadwood had never failed to distract him from his business and family life. The Star and Bullock Hardware Store was thriving in a two-story wooden building on the corner of Main and Wall Street, Deadwood. He was still happily married to Martha, and they were building themselves a good life in the once-wild mining camp that was now rapidly turning into the biggest city in Lawrence County, South Dakota. In fact, Martha had borne Seth two more surviving children: a little girl, Florence, and a little boy, Stanley.

Seth's career as a lawman was also by no means stagnant. While he no longer carried the title of sheriff, he was made a deputy in Medora, North Dakota.

However, it was his business that would truly expand during the 1880s and 1890s. By 1881, Seth and Sol were ready to take the next step. They pooled their resources and purchased an enormous ranch together on the confluence of the Belle Fourche River and a nearby creek. The acres upon acres of beautiful arable land were soon put to use raising cattle and thoroughbred horses. To feed his livestock, Seth decided to plant a crop that was well known back East: alfalfa. This high-protein roughage crop has become the staple of livestock feeds across the world today, but Seth was the first to ever plant it in South Dakota. Today, the state produces several million tons of alfalfa every year.

While Seth was enjoying tending his ranch, his political career was far from over. Soon, he would meet a man who would become one of his dearest friends and also one of the most powerful influences on his life and career.

* * * *

Theodore Roosevelt was a broken man in 1884.

Thirteen years Seth's junior, Theodore, who hated being called Teddy, hadn't had an easy childhood. Asthma and other health issues had made his childhood a nightmare, and it was only when he discovered how much physical activity and fitness improved his symptoms that he was finally rid of terrifying nightmares of suffocating in his sleep. The same year that Seth came to Deadwood, Theodore went to Harvard and later lost his beloved father in 1878.

Despite these struggles, Theodore's career was promising in every way by 1884. He was thirty years old and had already proven himself an excellent writer with numerous published books; his capability as a strategist was evident, he had been elected to the New York State Assembly, and he was married to Alice Hathaway Lee.

On Valentine's Day, 1884, everything fell apart for Theodore. His first child had just been born two days earlier. The pregnancy and childbirth had proved too much for his treasured Alice, who died from kidney failure; on the very same day, Theodore's last surviving parent, his mother Mittie, also passed away in the same house.

Theodore's world was torn instantly to pieces. He is quoted as having said that his life had fallen apart. While he was still active politically in New York, Theodore had to find solace somewhere. He remembered an 1883 hunting trip during which he had visited South Dakota. Something about the harsh beauty of the Black Hills had captivated him, and he thought he could find peace and healing somewhere under that wide blue sky.

Theodore invested in a ranch near Medora and moved there, hoping to turn it into a business opportunity. The ranch would ultimately not succeed, but it did turn Theodore into a roping, range-riding cowboy over the next two years. And it introduced him to one of his closest friends and a man for whom he had endless respect.

At the time, Seth, who was a deputy in the area, was hot on the trail of yet another criminal. With more than a decade's experience as a

Wild West lawman, he had become a force to be reckoned with, the veteran of many a tense stand-off and violent arrest. He was riding across the hills seeking a horse thief known only as Crazy Steve.

Theodore, who had been interested in community leadership in Medora since his arrival, was also hunting for the same horse thief. He spent weeks chasing after Crazy Steve, sleeping on the ground and riding all day, and he was a scruffy figure when he spotted an intimidating figure approaching him.

Seth was the picture of a hard-eyed sheriff. His six-foot height was topped by gray eyes that, in the words of his grandson, could stare down a mad bull. When he met Theodore, however, he was as courteous as ever, and Theodore was instantly inspired by the man. They went searching for Crazy Steve together, cementing a friendship that would last for the rest of their lives, even after Theodore sold his ranch in 1886.

* * * *

When he wasn't chasing after horse thieves with interesting nicknames, Seth was expanding his business. A golden opportunity came to him in 1890—nine years after purchasing the Star and Bullock Ranch Company.

At the time, railroads were spreading out across the West like spiderwebs, linking the many boom towns together and enabling trade to build them into real cities instead of mining camps. By then, the land had been neatly parceled out and sold, so the railway companies had no choice but to buy large tracts of lands on which to lay their tracks. They were interested in laying a railroad to Minnesela, South Dakota, a town very close to the S&B Ranch Company, and a nearby speculator quoted them a truly exorbitant amount of money to buy enough land for it.

Seth and Sol, the partners-in-crime that they were (figuratively—by all accounts, their business was always above board), immediately pounced on this opportunity. They offered the Fremont, Elkhorn, and Missouri Valley Railroad forty acres of land at no charge at all but with one caveat: instead of building the station in Minnesela, the railroad company was asked to build it on the ranch itself, about five miles from the town.

Given the prospect of free land, the railroad company immediately accepted. The station was built near the Belle Fourche River, and Seth started offering free land to anyone who would start a business near the station. Within months, Minnesela had waned in importance, and buildings were springing up on this part of Seth's ranch. It wasn't long before the town of Belle Fourche had sprung up like a colony of mushrooms almost overnight, and fueled by Seth's and Sol's astute business sense, it constantly grew in size and importance. Soon, it became the county seat and one of the largest railheads in the entire United States.

Seth, Martha, the two girls, and little Stanley were still living in Deadwood at this time, and the Star and Bullock Hardware Store remained an integral part of their livelihood. Even after a devastating fire swept through Deadwood in 1879, burning down hundreds of buildings (including the Gem Variety Theater, although it was rapidly rebuilt), the Star and Bullock store survived and continued to thrive.

It was not so lucky in 1894. A blazing inferno swept once again through the town, and this time, the Star and Bullock store was not spared from the wrath of the blaze. It burned to the ground aside from a small brick storeroom.

Sol and Seth decided that the time for a mere hardware store was over. Deadwood was a very different town than the mining camp they had entered eighteen years before. It was no longer a place where gold miners went; now, it was a bustling city, filled with commerce and even tourism, and Seth decided it was high time that a reputable counterpart to the Gem Variety Theater was built. Instead of rebuilding their hardware store, they were going to build a hotel.

It took two years and many, many blocks of pink and white sandstone, but by 1896, the Bullock Hotel was complete—and it was a marvel. With three floors filled with opulent luxuries, the Bullock Hotel was a place of genteel culture, a world away from the raunchy world of the Gem. It boasted a grand lobby, a vast dining room, and even a sample room for use by the many salesmen who came to Deadwood—and all that only on the ground floor. The other two floors contained sixty-three luxurious rooms kitted out with oak dressers and brass bedsteads, en-suite bathrooms, and even a balcony and library. The whole thing was decorated in an Italian-Victorian style that would have befitted a hotel in the tamer reaches of the East. For the Wild West, the Bullock Hotel was a rare jewel.

In fact, to this day, guests can enjoy beautiful décor and endless luxuries at the very same Bullock Hotel, still located on the corner of Main and Wall Street in the city of Deadwood. While many of its amenities have obviously been upgraded, the Bullock Hotel still retains its historic charm.

Arguably, while Seth is better known for his exploits as a county sheriff, the Bullock Hotel was his real passion. He was an elegant host and enjoyed serving his guests. It was the apple of his eye, his pride and joy.

* * * *

In 1898, still licking its wounds after the American Civil War less than forty years earlier, the now-reunited United States' mettle would be tested in its first international conflict since the Civil War.

Cuba, the tiny island to the south of the US, had been embroiled in a bloody revolutionary war since 1895. Cuba was still a Spanish colony at the time, and the Spanish were subjecting native Cubans (many of them of mixed-race heritage) to appalling oppression. The United States quietly supported the Cuban rebels, but it had not yet actually joined the war.

All that changed on February 15th, 1898. The USS *Maine* had been lying quietly at anchor in Havana Harbor when it suddenly and violently exploded during the night, killing hundreds of men. A perfect storm of yellow journalism and long-standing tensions between the Old World and the United States resulted in a bitter conflict that would become known as the Spanish-American War.

Theodore's political career had by then taken off in a big way. He had become the New York City police commissioner in 1894, and in 1897, he was appointed the assistant secretary of the US Navy.

However, it was not as the assistant secretary of the Navy that Theodore would serve in the Spanish-American War. Theodore wanted to fight with his boots on the ground. He promptly resigned from his position and put together a volunteer cavalry regiment that would make him famous: the 1st United States Volunteer Cavalry, better known as Roosevelt's Rough Riders.

Seth never saw active duty, but he had maintained his friendship with Theodore, and he was quick to volunteer. While he wasn't part of the Rough Riders themselves, he joined another US volunteer cavalry regiment and traveled all the way down to Louisiana for training, earning the rank of captain of Troop A during training.

The war, however, did not last long enough to benefit from Seth's leadership. Although the Spanish American-War was officially ended on December 10th, 1898, the last battle had been fought on July 17th. The war lasted less than three months, and Seth returned home to Deadwood.

In 1899, Theodore's political career had nearly reached its zenith. The vice president at the time, Garret Hobart, died unexpectedly of heart failure. Although Theodore was reluctant to take the position, he was eventually made vice president of the United States under President William McKinley. This fateful choice would catapult him into the most powerful position in the country just two years later. When President McKinley was assassinated at a convention in

September 1901, Theodore, the scruffy, unshaven cowboy that Seth had met in South Dakota, became the president of the United States of America.

For America, Theodore's presidency meant, among many other things, an increased emphasis on conservation. Part of South Dakota's Black Hills—Seth's home for twenty-five years—had been made a reserve, and Theodore considered that there was no one better than Seth to become the forest supervisor of it. He always maintained his deep respect for Seth, even though Seth was just a lowly businessman and sheriff. Nonetheless, Theodore called him an example of a true frontiersman.

This became more obvious than ever in 1905. Theodore had served for four years as the US president simply because he had been in the right position at the right time; in 1904, however, he was elected president in his own right. The inauguration took place in 1905, and Seth was deeply proud of his friend. He ordered fifty cowboys to get ready for Theodore's inaugural parade. They were a testimony to the influence that Dakota's wilderness had had on Theodore, and they were a spectacular sight as they rode down the street with silver on their hand-tooled saddles and their six-shooters flashing in their holsters, led by Seth Bullock and his steely-eyed stare.

Considering that Seth had tamed Deadwood, it was little surprise that Theodore made him a US marshal the same year that he was inaugurated. Seth would serve in his treasured home of South Dakota until 1914.

Although Seth was sixty-five years old by this time and had led a very long and busy life, this by no means meant retirement for the aging sheriff. When the First World War broke out, Theodore, who was no longer president but rather a Nobel Peace Prize laureate for his role in mediating the end of the Russo-Japanese War, appointed eighteen officers to raise a volunteer regiment to assist on the French front in 1917. Unsurprisingly, one of these officers was Seth Bullock. He threw himself into the task, but it was all in vain. President

Woodrow Wilson never approved the volunteer regiments, and they were disbanded before the end of the war.

For both Seth and Theodore, this was the beginning of the end.

Sol Star, who had been Seth's staunch friend since the Helena days (nearly forty years), was growing old. He had never married; Seth was the closest thing to family that he had. He lived on the S&B Ranch Company while Seth lived in Deadwood, and they remained good friends. Still, no friendship between mortals can last forever. Sol died in October 1917 at home on the ranch he loved. Seth gave him a funeral in Deadwood, which was, according to some accounts, "fit for a president." Sol had been one of the most influential citizens that Deadwood ever had.

Theodore was still young in comparison; by January 1919, he was only sixty years old and still as healthy as a horse, at least to all appearances. Tragically, his death would be unexpected. He was feeling a little unwell on the evening of January 5th, 1919, but he went to bed as usual. However, he would never rise again. He suffered a pulmonary embolism—a blood clot that affects the lungs—and died that evening.

His death was an awful blow to Seth. Having lost both Sol and Theodore, Seth grieved deeply and intensely. All he could think of was dedicating a monument to Theodore, displaying the deep mutual respect that the two men had held for one another. Helped by some fellow Black Hills residents, Seth erected a monument facing a nearby mountain, which was renamed Mt. Roosevelt. It was unveiled on the Fourth of July, 1919.

After a lifetime of chasing crooks and taming the Wild West, it wasn't a bullet that ultimately ended Seth's life. Unlike Wild Bill, he didn't die from a bullet to the brain. Instead, he passed away peacefully at home in the town he had helped to tame. Belle Fourche might have been the town he built, but Deadwood would always be his home, and he died there from colon cancer on September 23rd, 1919.

Conclusion

The Wild West is undoubtedly one of the most fascinating periods in the history of the United States of America. From the illustrious cowboy to the snaggle-toothed outlaw to the steely-eyed lawman, it is peopled with characters who loom larger than life. Romanticized though it may be, it was a brutal time for many, a testimony to the extent of human depravity and an example of the violence of which mankind is capable.

Yet among all of these hard characters and frontier lawmen, Seth Bullock stands out not for his sternness, nor for his marksmanship skills, nor for any kind of legendary exploits or brutality. He stands out for traits that were undervalued in the Old West yet shine in the modern day: his honesty, integrity, intense loyalty to his friends and family, and the capability of using a difficult childhood not as a fuel for a life of crime but as a springboard to greater things.

In the time of the Wild West, Seth Bullock had succeeded in taming the one thing that most Western men—notably those who so willingly patronized Al Swearengen's Gem Variety Theater—never managed to rope or break. These men captured wild horses and bucked them till they broke, yet they never succeeded in taming themselves.

But Seth Bullock was a man in complete command of himself. And it was his ability to control his own desires, his own fears, and his own flaws that made him the man who tamed Deadwood.

More than one hundred years after the death of Seth Bullock, Deadwood has become a thriving city. Its colorful history attracts tourists from all over the world, with many of them staying at the Bullock Hotel. And perhaps Seth, even in death, couldn't quite bring himself to let go of the town that made him who he was. Some say that if one of the servers stands idle for just a few minutes too long in the Bullock Hotel, the ghost of Seth Bullock walks the halls once again, ready to ensure that justice will always be done.

Here's another book by Captivating History that you might like

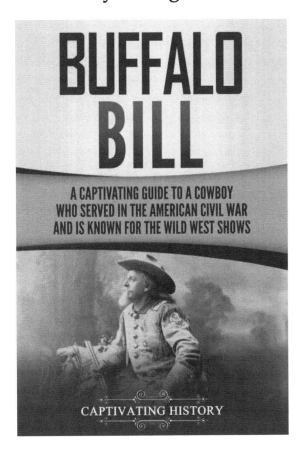

Free Bonus from Captivating History (Available for a Limited time)

Hi History Lovers!

Now you have a chance to join our exclusive history list so you can get your first history ebook for free as well as discounts and a potential to get more history books for free! Simply visit the link below to join.

Captivatinghistory.com/ebook

Also, make sure to follow us on Facebook, Twitter and Youtube by searching for Captivating History.

Sources

Historic Bullock Hotel website: https://www.historicbullock.com/

Deadwood City website: http://www.deadwood.com/

Weiser, K. 2019, *Seth Bullock – Finest Type of Frontiersman*, Legends of America, viewed 1 February 2021, <https://www.legendsofamerica.com/we-sethbullock/>

Holtzmann, R. 2013, *Mr. Bullock Goes to Washington*, South Dakota Magazine, viewed 1 February 2021, <https://www.southdakotamagazine.com/mr-bullock-goes-to-washington>

Boardman, M. 2019, *Bullock: No Bull*, True West, viewed 1 February 2021, <https://truewestmagazine.com/seth-bullock/>

History.com Editors 2020, *Theodore Roosevelt*, A&E Television Networks, viewed 1 February 2021, <https://www.history.com/topics/us-presidents/theodore-roosevelt>

Roberts, P., *Agnes Thatcher Lake: Equestrian Rider, Circus Performer, and Wild Bill's Wife*, Wyoming Almanac, viewed 1 February 2021, <http://wyomingalmanac.com/buffalo_bones_stories_from_wyomings_past_1978-2015/wife_of_wild_bill_agnes_thatcher_lake>

Finding Dulcinea Staff 2011, *On This Day: Wild Bill Hickok Kills Davis Tutt in a Duel,* Finding Dulcinea, viewed 1 February 2021, <http://www.findingdulcinea.com/news/on-this-day/July-August-08/On-this-Day--Wild-Bill-Hickok-Duels-Davis-Tutt.html>

Weiser, K. 2020, *Rough & Tumble Deadwood, South Dakota*, Legends of America, viewed 1 February 2021, <https://www.legendsofamerica.com/sd-deadwood/>

Carlson, G. 2014, *Roosevelt's Contemporaries: Seth Bullock*, Theodore Roosevelt Center, viewed 1 February 2021, <https://www.theodorerooseveltcenter.org/Blog/Item/Seth%20Bullock>

Deadwood, S. D. Revealed website: www.deadwood.searchroots.com

Weiser, K. 2020, *Al Swearengen & the Notorious Gem Theater*, Legends of America, viewed 1 February 2021, <https://www.legendsofamerica.com/we-gemsaloon/>

Biography.com Editors 2020, *Wild Bill Hickok Biography,* A&E Television Networks, viewed 1 February 2021, <https://www.biography.com/personality/wild-bill-hickok>

History.com Editors 2020, *Wild Bill Hickok is Murdered*, A&E Television Networks, viewed 1 February

2021, <https://www.history.com/this-day-in-history/wild-bill-hickok-is-murdered>

Weiser, K. 2019, *Solomon Star – A Natural Deadwood Leader*, Legends of America, viewed 1 February 2021, <https://www.legendsofamerica.com/sd-solstar/>

The National Parks Service website on Yellowstone National Park: https://www.nps.gov/yell/learn/historyculture/history-faqs.htm

Memmot, J. 2018, *Remembering a Rochester man's ill-fated journey to the Arctic*, Democrat & Chronicle, viewed 1 February 2021, <https://www.democratandchronicle.com/story/news/local/columnists/memmott/2018/08/01/remembering-rochester-mans-ill-fated-journey-arctic/871024002/>

Illustrations

Illustration II: Public Domain

https://commons.wikimedia.org/w/index.php?curid=1245
18

Illustration III: Photograph by Carol M. Highsmith

https://commons.wikimedia.org/wiki/File:The_Bullock_H
otel,_built_in_1886_by_Seth_Bullock,_the_Wild_West_t
own%27s_first_sheriff._Deadwood,_South_Dakota_LCC
N2011634118.tif

Made in the USA
Middletown, DE
10 July 2024

57106839R00033